disc

WEATHER WATCH

Summer

by Cynthia Amoroso and Robert B. Noyed

Summer is here! Summer is one of the four **seasons**. It comes after spring and before fall.

Summer is the third season of the year.

Summer is the hottest season. Many of the days are sunny, too. The sun shines late into the evening.

In the summer, the sun goes down later in the day.

Sometimes there are strong storms during summer. Thunder, lightning, and heavy rain are common during this time of year. Some storms might have **tornadoes**.

Lightning strikes during a summer storm.

The rain and sun help plants grow. Trees and bushes are full of leaves. Flowers **bloom** and show their many colors.

Flowers need water in the summer.

Many people take care of gardens in the summer. They grow tomatoes, beans, peas, carrots, and other vegetables. Many berries are ready to pick in the summer.

Berries are ready to eat in the summer.

Bees are very busy in the summer. They buzz from flower to flower. They make honey in their **hives**.

A bee flies to a flower.

Summer is a busy time. People like to go swimming, boating, and fishing. Many people go on **vacations** in the summer.

These children are having fun on their family vacation.

Camping is great in the summer, too. Campers **roast** hot dogs and marshmallows over campfires.

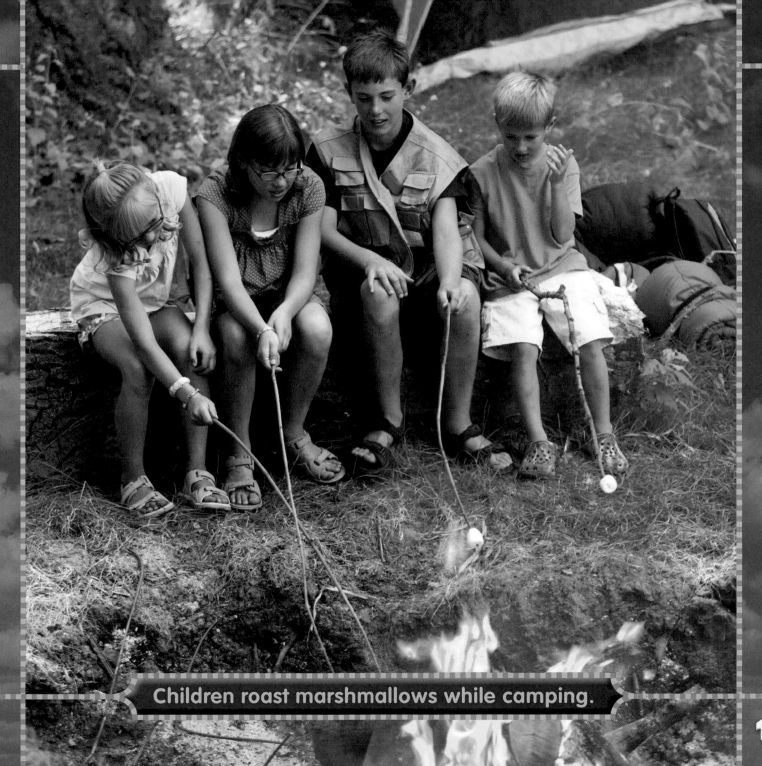

Children roast marshmallows while camping.

Many people enjoy summer picnics with family and friends. There are many **parades** that are fun to watch.

This parade celebrates the Fourth of July.

There are lots of things to do in the summer. Go outside and enjoy the sunny weather!

Sisters swing outside in the summer.

Glossary

bloom (BLOOM): When flowers open up, they bloom. Flowers bloom in the spring and summer.

hives (HYVZ): Hives are where bees live. Bees make honey in hives.

parades (puh-RAYDZ): Parades are when people march for holidays. The Fourth of July has lots of parades.

roast (ROHST): If people roast something, they cook it. Hot dogs can roast over a campfire.

seasons (SEE-zinz): Seasons are the four parts of the year. The four seasons are winter, spring, summer, and fall.

tornadoes (tor-NAY-dohz): Tornadoes are swirling tubes of air that come down from the sky. Tornadoes have high winds that can harm people and things.

vacations (vay-KAY-shunz): Vacations are time off from work or school to rest or to travel. Many families take vacations in the summer.

To Find Out More

Books
Branley, Franklyn M. *Sunshine Makes the Seasons*. New York: HarperCollins, 2005.

Roca, Nuria. *Summer*. Hauppauge, NY: Barron's, 2004.

Rockwell, Anne. *Four Seasons Make a Year*. New York: Walker & Co., 2004.

Web Sites
Visit our Web site for links about summer: *childsworld.com/links*

Note to Parents, Teachers, and Librarians: We routinely verify our Web links to make sure they are safe and active sites. So encourage your readers to check them out!

Index

bees, 12

camping, 16

fall, 2

flowers, 8, 12

parades, 18

plants, 8, 10

rain, 6, 8

spring, 2

storms, 6

sun, 4, 8, 20

vacations, 14

About the Authors

Cynthia Amoroso has worked as an elementary school teacher and a high school English teacher. Writing children's books is another way for her to share her passion for the written word.

Robert B. Noyed has worked as a newspaper reporter and in the communications department for a Minnesota school district. He enjoys the challenge and accomplishment of writing children's books.

On the cover: Many people go to the beach in the summer.

Published by The Child's World®
1980 Lookout Drive • Mankato, MN 56003-1705
800-599-READ • www.childsworld.com

ACKNOWLEDGMENTS
The Child's World®: Mary Berendes, Publishing Director
The Design Lab: Design and production
Red Line Editorial: Editorial direction

PHOTO CREDITS: David Franklin/iStockphoto, cover; iStockphoto, cover, 5, 11, 17; Elena Elisseeva/iStockphoto, 3, 9; Thomas Larsen/iStockphoto, 7; Sabrina Dei Nobili/iStockphoto, 13; Marzanna Syncerz/iStockphoto, 15; Sherri R. Camp/Shutterstock Images, 19; Eileen Hart/iStockphoto, 21

Printed in the United States of America in Mankato, Minnesota.
November 2009
F11460

LIBRARY OF CONGRESS CATALOGING-IN-PUBLICATION DATA
Amoroso, Cynthia.
  Summer / by Cynthia Amoroso and Robert B. Noyed.
    p. cm. — (Weather watch)
  Includes index.
  ISBN 978-1-60253-364-6 (library bound : alk. paper)
  1. Summer—Juvenile literature. I. Noyed, Robert B. II. Title. III. Series.
  QB637.6.A46 2010
  508.2—dc22   2009030219